THE
GENERATION
NEW POET SERIES

VOLUME I

Edited by George A. White

AND IN HIM, TOO; IN US

POEMS

AND IN HIM

By KONSTANTINOS LARDAS

Selected and Introduced by *AUSTIN WARREN*

TOO; IN US

Generation · *Ann Arbor*

ACKNOWLEDGMENTS   Thanks are due to the following periodicals in which certain of the poems in this volume first appeared, and who have kindly given permission for their inclusion here: *Accent, Athene, Crux, Harper's Bazaar, The Literary Review, Overture,* and *The Prairie Schooner* in America; *The Dalhousie Review* in Canada; *Krikos* in England; *Nea Hestia* in Greece. Similar thanks are due to the *Anthology of Magazine Verse for 1958* for permission to reprint "Paschals", and to the Borestone Mountain Poetry Awards *(Best Poems of 1962), (Best Poems of 1963)* for permission to reprint "With Open Love" and "Spartaric". The poem, "Sons Of All Fathers", was awarded the University of Michigan *Bain-Swiggett Poetry Award* for 1962.

Library of Congress Catalog card number: 64-25080

Printed in the United States of America.
Published by *GENERATION* under the authority of The Board in Control of Student Publications, The University of Michigan.

Published 4 July 1964
First Edition
Number 247 / 1500

for
Sofia

for

Sofia

CONTENTS

Introduction

The poems of Konstantinos Lardas are those of a young man who has taken from books and universities only what he needed and could use and whose gratuitous endowment is his lineage from an ancient people, makers of myths and philosophies.

Lardas' deeply intuitive and always oral and eloquent poetry is at the remotest extreme from the ingenuities and cerebral contrivances which pass, academically, for 'metaphysical'. His metaphysics is that of the pre-Socratic philosophers, with that special Greek continuity which combines the most archaic Hellenic thought about water, fire, and family with the most traditional and yet speculative form of Christian thought, that of Hellenic Orthodoxy.

I know of no such deeply intuitive, verbally enamoured, seawardly rhythmical poetry being written in English today. It is true—perhaps even great—poetry.

AUSTIN WARREN

18 March 1964

11

It is good to grow wise under sorrow

EUMENIDES 1:520

And In Him, Too; In Us

From the horizon of a higher roof,
I saw unending chain of angels
Winged with corrugated wings.

Sure-footed grippings of the slanted roof
Along precarious coping, brought them to gaping hole
From which rose emanating rays

Blurring the sun-reflecting corrugated sheets.
They cast their silver wings beside the opened hole.
Stripped angels preparing for the plunge.

Climbing the razored roofs, I came to mark the sheets.
The chain began again, the corrugated winging,
My father's father at the head.

He saw me and he winged himself one sheet
More heavy than the strongest man,
And proudly bore the breaking weight;

A non-obligatory load
For he was white-haired old; and we, his youngest blood,
Looked in amazement at his proud old age.

From the horizon of his higher self,
I saw drenched shoulders strain to break
Imprisoning chain as he squared sheets

Along the purlined roof to close the roaring hell.
To close and not to fall. To skirt above
The Rolling-Mill; to teeter, poise, to test.

14

He capped that hell with metal sheets.
His was the final capping, obliterating fire.
Yet hell was even where he walked.

It stung the purlins from the rolling steel,
It scorched the outstretched wings,
And from the vents, on him, its hottest tongues stretched out.

Still, by the ladder, ready to descend,
He smiled, for he was proud of us, his youngest blood,
And prouder still, of his own burning years.

And in that hell was heaven flaming also;
Under him, and on. And heaven's conflagration
Entered in him, too; and burned its mark in us.

Until Consumed

What comes with crushing of a face?

What whumping noise
Eases releases hurtles
Compressor gage

To wrack ream bonefleshblood
Stubbled and torn out hairs
Wrenching and reeling nerves
Plundering writhing all?

Sounds sights thoughts thunder stop.

Swooped dying of the whirring noise
Marks masks blanks startled face.
And O and Ah and we who never saw
Who never heard the roaring noise?

Sound of exploding steel
Sucks thwucks
Sounds and resounds in us
Wracks wreaks and whacks in us

Ever will sound will suck.

II

What comes with crushing of a man?

Quiet the widow numb
Besieged by brother's words
Spung lipped

Screams scouring sounds
Sacking and scourging those who stand
To shove her shaking to the couch
Strangling and struggling all.

Sounds sights thoughts rumble blast.

Spun crying plunges to her limbs
Rouses the jostled body.
Writheful and wrathful wracking
Spurs sparging screams.

A jagged and a jousting surging
Pounded by three men sitting and rising
Falling heavy on with my ravaged aunt
Constrain her sinewed soul

That would lunge leap to hell.

III

What comes with crushing of a face?

Doped needles pierce
Not bind spasmodic swarfing.
Spartarizmátic

Stingings of my ears
Hold cries not cringe
Before unstinted words
Brother beleaguered swords of love.

Sounds sights thoughts sunder swerve.

She never heard how friends pushed
Back the bleeding eyes or saw them
Penny closed that could no longer see.
And through glazed peering and bizarre

Sees only artful now wax powdered chilled
Her pillaged man her panic parted groom.
Now only manic calls
"Bird Angel Child O Golden One".

Stunned sphygmic abolition.

IV

What comes with crushing of a man?

Years black robed range.
Dreamed rage at attic window
Lights crackled

Body as I come to succor her
Widowed by faulty our machine
Our gage that blundered in his face
Buffeting her all anguish and all pain.

Sounds sights thoughts stumble speed.

Yet soul screams begs release.
Loathes me? Bares breasts to me
Wrinkled and dugged dug now by none
But by her fingers nipples stung

And O and Ah and me my spluttered mouth
Spurts spills with souring milk.
Gaged death loud long implacable resounds.
And I I drink have drunk will drink all guilt

Until I gouged consumed I I I dumbled die.

Wanting

After great feasting,
After much dancing
And displays of love
Comes quick the hour of return.

A peasant girl
Allays our fearful journey
By her songs.

Our new-found cousins
In young awareness
Of their manhood,
Their great pride,

Lead us,
The worldly, bitter lords,
Past the ancestral paths,
Along ancestral slabs
Which constitute the island roads.

Now, through our veins,
Flow night,
Dark Prámnian wine.

Our feet must stumble
On the paths, as we go,
Arm in arm, to home.

We two, reigning alone,
Sucking cold air,
Revive;
Can slowly mount,
Can count the steps.

Once more,
In glowing tower
Of the ancestral home,
We are the bridegroom and the bride.

And now, before the window,
Beside the wooden couch,
Below the fern-encrusted icon,

Our lamp
Burns waiting, low;
Our love
Burns bright and wanting.

Largess

Throned on her bed,
Weighted by homespun black,
Most ancient goddess,
She who had been a queen,

Upright,
Defiant,
Whirled round to greet us;
We who had crossed the seas.

White, whitest beauty
Of her wrinkled face
Lighted
The homespun black,

Made joyous our first meeting.
Fondling our arms, our hair,
She offered us her blessing;
Plucked from beneath her pillow

The largest largess
Of her fruits;
A blazing pomegranate
Bleeding in open hands.

She who was once a queen,
A goddess to her village
Offered us joys, as multitudinous
As the seeds of this full fruit.

She, she remembered,
She counted all her joys.
My young bride kissed
The red fruit to her breasts

More gracious in this hovel
With this gift
Than on our
Virgin night.

Later, across the seas,
The proclamation of her death arrived.
We, we remembered.
We remember all our joys.

Sons Of All Fathers

Thrice blessed, along the shore we wade,
I, and Sofia, and remain afraid.
Once, be a blessing, but to have three sons
Shatters beyond belief; stuns
Infinitely storming raid.

You, who permitted us these sons,
Show us, upon what thumping drums
To strike, upon what dreams
To strum, that swelling screams
Blazingly blot all suns.

Thrice blessed, pontifically we walk
Baptizing deepest waters to rock
Our sons as once Sofia cradled
Them in her. Straddled
On backs, armhung, sons, seas embark.

We, who petition you to swim,
Smile as you cry to brim
The swollen sea; hear as you ear the sea
Sounding for fish, for waves; see
You swarm, plumb, plunge grim.

Thrice blessed, tides swarming sweep
Green seaweeds blanketing deep
Fears that seep and hold
And seadrum bind. Seaweeded, bold,
Hands, seize, upleap.

You, who direct upstrumming of our hands,
Dangle them high above the headlands
Of their souls; command their coronated
Grooming; bless seaweeds sated
By their glory; strike laureled bands.

Thrice blessed, imperially they shine.
Churchly coronas, orangeblossomed, line
Their heads; green halos burn to gold;
And myrtled icons blaze, fold
In filigreed, in fingered brine.

We, who our sons hallow haloidally,
Hawk to crowned kisses laughingly;
Drink splendid salt from limbs that dart
To be free from limbs; smile as they start,
Strike, drum, thud, run, storm splashingly.

Thrice blessed, we stand; and stand the seas.
Thrice blessed, they walk; and walk the lands that seize
And hold their thumping, drumbling cries.
Thrice blessed, imperially crowned and prized,
All stand, all walk; sons of all fathers of all seas.

Orestes Helioúmenos

for my son, Orestes

My helmet's plumes amaze you?
They are not living things to harm.
Fear me, fear warrior's arm,
But know, I go in terror,
Valor compels me forth
To guard Andromache and you.

Disarm? I cannot but go forth.
Skulls, warriors' arms, the stream
Will wither at your destined end.
Within these walls confined,
Yourself, Andromache bind.

There,
Touch those magic motes.
Lined by their spreading ray,
Stand in illumined, dazzling nudity.
I have not seen, I have not known
Such sun since I was young.

Gaze not on me,
Nor helmet's plumes,
Nor bold Andromache;
But to the gull's,
The sun's alarm take heed.

You were a sun-mote once,
Enthralling these,
Adorning other walls.
Lost in a pouting, slow awakening,
Orestes, stand and grasp that ray
Lighting the silence of these halls.

Child, be, as Scamándrios, amazed!
Soon, sprouting,
You shall know its terror. Grasp it,
But do not let it tear you
As innocent Astyanax was torn.

Orestes Helioúmenos,
Born of the magic motes,
Be ever bathed in light.

On Wildest Seas

White earth, eye stretching, wide,
Bound by the rain and snow
Bundle these weeds that hide
Bounding from frozen glow.

Blue grey and plush as weeds
Found in these campus seas
Sunder the slushy reeds
Slashing my footsteps' breeze.

White earth, eye stretching, wide,
Sound that I sloshing make
Hold to your pitted side
Sounding an ocean's quake.

Blue grey and plush as weeds
Pout of my steps on seas
Swells as the scattered seeds
Sprouting to starry sheaves.

White earth, eye stretching, wide,
Seagalleys crumble to my walk
And no warm seas abide
Slushing or solemn stalk.

Blue grey and plush as weeds
I walk on rain and snow
Wonder who speaks and bleeds
Calming the windwaves' blows.

White earth, eye stretching, wide,
Caught in these earthbreaks'
Sounds I ride
Swirling in silver seaquakes.

Blue grey and plush as weeds
I tremble to the needs. Lord, see.
Lord, bless my naked reeds.
Root them to earth. Launch them
On wildest seas.

Sea Risen

From the bleak Páphian coast we saw her;
We marveled at her rising . . .

First,
Land-devouring waves
Swirled to a roaring vortex
Sucking a passing trireme
To its depths;

So vastly grown, the whirlpool threatened us,
The moorage of our island.

Then,
Satiated,
Swollen to quiet foaming,
Released two praying, upraised arms,
Forth from its foam;

Revealed the gasping
Aphrodite.

After her struggles with the waves,
Her rising through the foam,
Her gleaming, golden tresses
Showered her naked bosom,
Her navel, with their light.

No longer bleak;
A paradise of light was Páphos.

We, singing our praises of her beauty,
Ran to the shore,
Cried of her wónderous
Rising from the sea.

Now, Páphos and all that foaming shore
Lie in aphótic regions:

Moored to the depths
By greater horrors
Than those of the land-devouring waves
Which drowned the passing vessel and its crew,
Spewed forth a golden queen.

A darker evil now,
For waves are cruel but true.

Swirling to Páphian coast,
The roaring vortex of an alien host
Sucks at the moorage of our island.
Sea-risen, golden Aphrodite,
Becalm these wilder seas;

Unite your mother, Cyprus,
With her only self.

Ómphalos

The frantic Sibyl
Scraped the spewed marrow from her arms
Flung it to earth;
Raved at the greatest god.

Blood, feathers and the eagles' claws
Streamed from the skies
Defiled the Delphic priestess.

Zeus, bloody-fingered,
Loosing the birds
To soar in his white heavens,
Tore out their piercing eyes.

Those blinded augurers,
Colliding in the universe,
Marked, with their fallen entrails,
The navel of the earth:

The firm-rimmed,
Love-defining Delphi.

Sputniks and Vanguards,
Sleek, wingless birds,
Stream to the higher skies
Crashing beyond Olympus.

These blinded messengers of man
Soar past the eastern cupolas
Shoot past white shaft of stone
Guarding the great Potomac.

No single frantic Sibyl curses now.
Now all the world sings of the
Singeing craters.

Where shall we mark the center,
The firm, omphálic navel of the universe?
Once, it was Delphi and her treasures;
Now, it is man; his love.

Anabasis

What was the sight of sea
To them
Was this still silent clearing
To my father's eyes.

Had we been climbing
To some sacred shrine,
Had we been scaling cliffs
As vanguards of a legion,

Our pilgrimage had not been
More devout,
Our band, less eager
For the battle.

Strange caravan;
My father mounted
On a careful beast,
A king;

And we,
The honor guard,
Surrounding him on foot,
Trailing the steep ascent.

Steep though the path had been,
Blue though the sea had shone
From that great height,
We, august, followed on,

Mindful of every jogging step
The beast had made
Lest it disturb
Our father.

A king may weary of his rule.
A man may have the world
And yet grow
Sick for home.

His tightening of the reins,
The donkey's soulful braying
Spoke our arrival
To his home,

Revealed
The silent clearing.
Stone walls, two rooms,
Had been a palace once.

Father,
Should we have known?
No, not
The Sea! The Sea!

These gnarled trees,
These heaped-up stones,
This silence
Was your home.

Father,
Should we have
Better known
Your heart?

God,
Who would have thought
To see the mounted king
Weep tears!

Spearman

As he were Zeus
Casting a fiery bolt
From white Olympus,
Dark lover of the sea
Poised on the rocky shore
Let fly his slender spear.

And by that ruse
Of ocean's sucking of the spear,
We, from the heights were drawn,
Down to the shore, to him.

So to seduce
Our innocence, our guilt,
Severed the distant poise;
Giving nor word, nor sign,
But the retrieving of the spear
Which yielded up a furtive

Octopus—
No greater than the heinous head
Of that dark lover of the sea,
Whose sinewy arms

Began to loose
All hardness from the scaly tentacles:
This, by his mighty arms' sacrificially
Swift dashing of the monster to the rocks.
Black stones wetted by the frothy foam
Live in remembrance of that piercing.

By that insatiable, odious deed
Reduced the flesh to pliant tenderness.
Away, and fix our gaze on upright spear
Implanted in the sand.

Spearman, Zeus Ominous,
We are before you on the strand.
The piercing, the amazed watch,
The slaughter and our guilt must end.
Dark lover, what is it from the sea,
What is it you retrieve, you punish?

A scaly absolution, blackened Zeus?
Spearman, we suppliants beg watch.
White foaming evil on the sand prostrates us,
And wills the gleaming rocks burn bright.

Alexander Agonistes

*In Troy, Alexander honored Achilles
by running races round his barrow.*

I

Hushed is the plain of Troy
As noble Alexander flaunts his strength,
Once more runs round the walls.

Broken, the brooch's tongue.
The chlámys falls.

"Circle the plain, circle the plain again,
    circle the plain.

Dark tomb-motes swell my lungs
Whose pain is song of speed.
To be the wind, the wild gale levelling the brush,
These walls, even this naked flesh cast off!
Black ribbon only binds my brow.

Now, Oh, embrace the quivering walls
Which yet exude the giant grief of Priam.

Pursuing and pursued,
I chase not Hector,
But all eluding life.

O, Peleus, that you had borne
from sea-spray such a one!
Thetis, come once again from sea-weeds;
Pray and adorn the ground
With tears for what is done.

My life's blood, glistening by gall,
Surges to flood of atavistic proof.

38

Black ribbon, bind beaded
Forehead like a thong,
And hold me to the chase.

"How many times, how many times again,
   how many times.

I rip you off, my mourning,
And I exalt in bitter agony for Him.
Black ribbon tears the ground;
Black ribbon flies and frees me
To honor Him, Achilles.

I have known love,
Known all its swollen wonders.

Perceiving and perceived,
When that love stopped,
All living stopped for me.

Throng,
Hoplites,
Marvel at your king!
Strong women,
Hold your heads,
Remembering to sing
Of grovellings in the nights!"

II

Lost is the leader now in Troy.
Gaunt shadow trails his strength
As myriad bodies strain the walls.

Broken, the noble stride.
He staggers and he falls.

"Show them the pain, show them the pain again,
   show them the pain.

Daring to conquer earth,
Daring to hope and think on birth,
Across His bier am I lain;
Miring the earth with rivulets of hair,
Maddened by pride.

Is that the wail of Hecuba?
Pour out titanic grief for me.

Pursuing and pursued,
The Furies bind me here
To brood upon my fate.

My heel, O Peleus, is bared.
Thetis, bathe me in brine;
Drape sea-weeds on my limbs
As once you cleansed Achilles.
Deign the comingling of our tears for the slain.

Achilles, mourn Patroclus.
Dumb dice are left to us.

Is that the wail of Hecuba?
No, my wild woman, swollen,
Wails for me and laughs.

"Tell them no more, tell them no more again,
   tell them no more.

No, not a man,
A lone dog foaming in dust am I,
Glowing with sweat,
Flowing in atavistic proof
To honor Him, Achilles.

Oh, I had not
Great love!

White gulls above me fly
And I would spear them
Would my love not die.

Child,
Son
Of my wailing amazon,
Emerge!
Riled by my fate,
Run to your Dawn,
Flailing your bronzed arms!"

Paschals

Lamb
Gifted by tenant farmer
For our feasting
Is now too beautiful for slaughter;

We caress it,
Wind ribbons round its holy head.

Who would dare sweep the knife across its throat?

Now lift it high;
Gift it, in turn,
Still breathing life,
To Gregory
Who clutches at his heart.

This be our paschal gift
To one who was a shepherd
In his youth.

Make his heart glad,
O lamb.

II

The lamb
Is now become the ram
To share the second Easter
With its master.

Cross-legged upon the bed he dreams.
Sail silver caiques round his hoary head.

Who would dare stop his fondling of the sheets?

Upon the bed,
His knotted hands mend nets,
Repair the masts
As he awaits
The final Easter.

Death be the paschal gift
To one who hungered for the winds'
White waves.

Sheep, multiply for him;
Masts, swell.

Pantokrátor

at Daphni, near Athens

What a great God
Was hidden in that dome!
Taut-fingered, gaunt-faced God
Welled, to my lips, the foam.

Once, fingers felt a likeness to that God;
Stretching to brow,
Seeping to living bone, to skull,
Swelling to vaunted home.

This, this is in me, awed;
This passion wrought by gall.
Held in the golden eye of the mosaic dome,
Crawl you, the Christ, or I?

See the vast cupping
Between the domed,
The sprawling ones below?
So is the space between us

Infinite as God.
Remembering our purposeful entombment,
Know, I await your coming,
As I await the coming of a God.

Eimí

Womb within womb within womb

World wombed
O loomed in stars
Though I lay oorie frozen
Contending with the dolphin and the snake
When on his temple only
Should be all coupling oréctic
Nor laughter sounds nor smiles
But heaving only heaving

Twin mountain wombed
Temple and I creation
In boulder fury flamed
Brighter than sun deeper than deepest gorge
Wound bound swoon flung exposed
To lower and to darker thrust
Of fronted mountain or of man
In burning only burning

Earth's sun sea's child
Seize center me to them
While pitted slab cold holds
Splayed genitalia on cold stone
Throed in throned crush of chanting snake
Charged surgings twirling flash
As purge the threnodies of blue mammalian fish
While dying only dying

O but endure the heaving
Fold arms or stretch outstretch
Now on back turned neck frenzied pulsed
To ádytum to holiest of holies
Nerves taut blood flood hung head
As to libation of curved throat
To sibyl laurel wound and by fumes framed
                    But swirling only swirling

Nor ewe nor snout-nosed being
Wild boar goat no nor lamb of God
Would stretch as I am stretched
Eyes bold bound beyond fuming
Vanquished dilate to vanished *E*
That heavy hung from columns once in wood
And once again in bronze and O in everlasting gold
                    In falling only falling

How was abducted letter then enduringly denied
How wrenched or wrung garroted
O centuries denied until *E* orphic
Is aborted fallen as were first temples here
Of laurel or of feather or of stone
That by fire wind and trembling fell
Beyond prophets to deny negate
                    While quaking only quaking

Now I I pronged in terror
Frozen to schístic slab core cleaved
Feel Gaea's fires sunder the silence of the *E*
Clutch mighty navel with conspiring palms
Grasp O thonged navel with corrupting hands
Navel that holds earth's writhing son entombed
Entombing earth release thronged stone
                    But clinging only clinging

That I might see fanged snake
That I might know
And hear not only clearest surging of
Castalian spring but hear
His slithery coming also unto me
And with pythónic strength
Crush me me crush who crush would crush
                    In wrapping only wrapping

E is eiréne wombing world
Nor seas nor mountains tumbling stars
Or brightest day or the defiled and hurled
From twin reflecting rocks or sound of hoof beats
On the stones or silver rustling of ten thousand
Thousand olive trees is need enough if
E be eiréne be eimí
                    While looming only looming

Throat arched to Him His Glory
Eyes reach to gore gorged in lone languishing
Of languid eagle soaring above last eyeburst lost
Wing tips edged furred in hazing sky
Not lost but seen retained
And hear not call or screaming sound
But sound of flapping only of in womb
                    But flapping only flapping

Soar soar with Him to Him
God of the sun and of the earth and of the
Underearth and of all water worlds
Genitor I I aulic rise twice shaking thunder roar
To save   Defiled I undefiled
Fly to contend again with python not now
As ravished child but reigning raging man
                    In rising only rising

O then to stand from stone
Wreathed all in dignity
To hold heart slack
Lure lead or luring bleed
O whóllily unknowing bring bless
To where peace reigns
Soul leaps
While standing only standing

Tomb within tomb within tomb

Once lay I O but stand now I
I who lay soared now stand
Bold wonder what

But in while what
Lord
Only this I know

One only man need cry eimí
And earth heeds vágitus
Vaginal trembles to the quickened word

And O that cry orífic
Sounds earth folds fills
Swells soars rends rips eimí

And holding this
Pontific O
Endures not lone
I am

Penúmbrial proclaims
Apógeal prevails
We are

                    *   *   *

Not longer now to speak of selves, of olive trees, of
eagles. No nor to speak of men who stumbled yesterday
through temples and along these paths to flee their broth-
ers' wrath . . .

For we were visitors to Greece.

Marvel on marvel overwhelmed. Exhausted to theatre
seats, we looked to fiercest nature; now ordered,—man-
comprehending, comprehensible.

Heads cocked, we wondered on circumscribing
spectacle of gendarmes, stiff-standing, arms angle-thrust,
rimmed militant to top-most circle of theatre. At other
temples, other shrines, flanked marble statues guarded.
But these? These were living stones. We thought them
added men; a splendid guard to Oedipus. Behind gendarmes, massed peasants who had climbed the mounded
hill to frame theatre curve.

Sporadically, the other tourists came, hunted their
Athens-ordered seats. Slowly they came, for time seemed
now suspended, irrevocable. Not time alone. The whole
world bowed, the whole world buckled to the silence and
hung to hold its bartered breath to hear the words of
Oedipus.

Ah, but as thunder roars, as flood whack-bursts to
dam, or, O, as earthquake roars, we shuddered to
overwhorling noise;—then startle-saw that it was surging
mass of men, of women, children, who had broken cross-
held arms of the gendarmes to pour into theatre. They
would not be contained. They would not be out-cordoned

                           49

or out-flung. They swarmed theatre as once the earth had sunder-crushed to bury temples and their land.

We, barbarous had come, usurping seats from them. They roared to overwhelm. And just as sudden was the silence.

Awed, not as in doming churches of the East where church is home, where man may smile to friends, and whisper, speak, or cry to sons; but hushed, as if, at last, in hovering Hagia Sophia, they sat in mutestation.

And clouded, clouted by the holiness, the silence, we felt a greater frenzy. We felt that mutilation too were promise. We felt that sudden might arise the writhing dance, the writhing line that led to sacrificial altars even, to vastest searing rites.

This, their inheritance: to know. Ours now: to want.

*   *   *

Plague of walled Thebes was ours by summoning of king. "Children!" he cried. "Sons! Daughters!" And plague of civil and of promised war, and plague of stunning love was ours by adumbration to the king. And we were suppliants too; quick-gazed on him who lone had solved the taloned riddle that tore Teiresias' heart. From king, begged absolution; king who stood absolute to us.

Too, and ourselves were emptied unto Oedipus, Jocasta. But we were plaintive sons to them through rooted choric foliation. And no, not Oedipus alone, by his magnificence, seared; no, nor Jocasta; but chorus seized and stormed,—seer-questers, bearded, draped,

50

sequestered in rigid and in flowing spontaneity. Balanced to ritual intensity, chorus constricted us; and we, and it, itself, became orchestral to Oedipus and to Jocasta.

Crystality of song, rigidity of pose, crypticity to horror and to joy, moved chorus now to stand, and now to hover and harangue, and now to break in python-writhing, —diaspora of men. And though dispersed to altar, and though, or dispossessed of tongue, and though, or dionysian obsessed, now, as if of, or, O, as if in ecstasy of grace, became the babbling many and the one,—immutest, allsublimest Om.

And we,—Sofia, I,—now primal man, now woman, wakened to world's first dawn, chant-wrothe to threshing-floor ledged in the clefted hill. And we, now, one, honored the gods, hoved man, in this, this holiest, uniquest place, —parthénic now, as if before the advent even of precursors, or even of the blunder-surging, sanguinary song of goat.

*   *   *

Chorus conceived Jocasta (Paxinoú). She rose full-nurtured, now more than woman; mother-wife. She rose to pummel-stun. Her ecstasy was ours; ours so much so, that from theatre, woman's screams retorted, struck Jocasta's ears. And she, Jocasta, one gaze cast, and silence-froze, and rooted her and us to her. Cast glare was convocation to consider kingly orbs of king,—eyes that conspired to hold.

"Unending night enshrouds you, and you can never harm me!" cried Oedipus to seer. "No! Nor can any man who gazes full in sun!" He who was man unto himself

51

was soon to walk the earth more wretched-wracked, supremest-pained to all. He who was man unto himself was god. Unending loathing soon to enshroud him, soon to eclipse forever his owned full-gazing into sun.

Autotimóric,—oedipal exhumations forecast, too, all that was promised him before his birth, the plunder-chaosed death of mother and of wife, the binding exodus from Thebes.

Oedipus (Minotís) stood now, now stood all vengeful and avenged; exilic now before the royal gate.

Eye-spillings, eye-gougings issued forth not lone excessively to blood that flooded face, that issue-gorged to chest;—mouth, too, his, boomed greater terror, terror of king, terror of man, of men.

Giant the mouth, giant the curse to Cithaeróna that held him not in infancy to die, but sent him flourishing to other land, and brought him home, exposed,—giant the lips that formed the caverned "O"—and O, that "O", echo of wail that from Cithaerónian cliffs sounded, resounded to our ears, and to beyond the olive forests, to Itéa, and to the Gulf of Corinth, and to all Greece, and to beyond, and to around and over cliffs, to North, to East, to West.

Scarred echo, sounded, resounded in the air, as if God dropped gigantic boulder in the ocean-air, sending reverberated soundings, air-circling-rings, resounding through the world.

And to our ears returned. And to our souls surrender-

plunged in first and final threnody of man, consuming us in his oedipal fire.

What anguish could be ours to come to his? And what our woes before the woes of Oedipus? Convulsed to mouth, we were incised in cratered sockets of the king.

Eyes, eyed agony of Jocasta; eyes, eyed and mouth, mouthed agony of Oedipus. Excess of pity and of terror exceeded those millions dead-pinioned to crag-canyons and to road that leads to Delphi and away,—excelled in horror those bucket-heaped abominations; eyes ripped and reaped and held as evidence by soldiers and gendarmes and citizens of Left, and citizens of Right, and citizens of War.

Greater than this, greater than lava-scorching curse, —that *purposed* emptying of eyes.

Deep, deep in us; deep and forever, we remember.

*   *   *

Holiness then was ours, hallowed by blooded agony that blunder-streamed to earth. Silence was ours, O, unendurably enduring.

Ah, and we knew that cries of all the men who were, and are, and are to be, were nothing, are nothing, shall ever be nothing, before this silence standing to Oedipus, looming to, of, and in, and for, all time.

Touching Sofia to the silence, and being touched by her to silence, we have been ever one in comprehension and in love.

This, our inheritance. Endow.

Sotéric

Not eden entrails slouched to mud
Not carcassed legs stiff-flung to clefted prayers
Not eyes quag-razed ears bogged
Not teeth mire-gleamed nor hoofs nor hollowed horns
Nor body putrified to sun

Not holy-Rabbi-seen forsaken disemboweled to Him

Nor vultures hovered no nor flies
Nor worms gut-revelled in quadrúped flesh
No no nor strident linger-stenched
Nor roared nor reared nor splung
But cool calm soft quicksanded sunk

All holy-Sóter-drowned and disembodied

II

Sepulchral chaos skied earthed and oceaned cast
Oceans of oceans plied skies bolted mountains spung
To sire parthénic cosmos in ourselves

Here glean how glean before snow-startled Yéros stream
That stumbles unto river Yéros unstoppable unbridged
Gaze now to hovering gerótic harnessing of cross

I to redeem I to reel petrified to Him
I to craze-gleam spire-raze to sons
Calling implacable untamed

Naming my O my eden O my carrion fears
"Death bubbles in the water sir death hides
Come father sir come see come touch the hidden hide"

Reed broke to touch reed poked to see
Jeweled pebbled bouldered goat that relic lay
Bold hung suspended to quick water quicker sand

And no not body pried to crossing feet
And no not steeped to gore not stepped
And no not bones to crumble-stoop to us

Stringent and rifted ever and ever inner-in
Incrouched to reaming torrent
Upward the goat-song sung

Ah and all shone all spied all reliquary white
Shining beyond putrescence
To sire parthénic cosmos in ourselves

III

Only sotéric-hand child-hand bird flew to mine
Only son-hand stunned mine cool circle-soared to breeze
Only mine not mine but wretch fire
Only to feather-surge as first in eden father wreathed and
    son
Winged hands pure hands adore

All holy-Rabbi-come see yes see and adorn enthrone

And son-led unto hump and father-shown and seen white
And cloud-curve back that contains all heavens
Yes yes and O beyond the gleaming and engulfing death
Yes glow to shine in waters swirled to swoop
Yes now lambed lioned roar-rouse to Zion soar

Yes holy-Sóter-chosen yes yes-chosen yes-enthralled

Rheátic

*"Then, from the bell-tower, turn left and
follow path to find your father's home".*
—*Ikaria 1962*—

I

Tau-thonged enshacklement of bell
Man-sized the seizing posts

In rudeness taued or oxened
where not bound beasts might plod

where not yoked men might walk
where not sieged sailors sail

Loom monolithic Egypt to my feet
course domed rear minaretted East

roar labyrinthined obelisks of home
nude golden-triangled and yorked

No not emplinthined glories
but threshing-floor incisement

of entongued obeisance
Bell-tower besiegement

not me not holiness outclang
Toll tideless pillorization mine

II

Mind to a fallen to a broken
Brook wild escragglements of brush

Enter untoldness of the fallen
to touch smooth

non-existent stones of olive press
to hail unfurled

beseechments of armless sails
that not wheat longer grind

Touch to retain
past clangor of the bell

past bondage
of the clogging wheat

past silence
of the pressing mill

past lefting path
And catabástic fall

III

Fallen to steepest deltaing of path
encompassant to sun
farest in dryness where not rays can pierce
but cataract but flood

Cascadancy to surge
to a downswooped invasion-down to hell

Not black-cragged flow stygéaned
not higher sourced and secretest
Supremest carry me alluvial
descendant quick to hell

Flooded and river-flushed
earth-borne or water-held
slow-chaosed glide
to harrowing of hell

Not coin-mouthed no to Styx
nor candle-kissed nor threnodied to brow
nor icon-scented to crossed hands
nor virgined flower-crowned

But sceptered now enwifed now and ensoned
And living
sundered suddenly from life
and rush-flung deep to topple to destroy

Fired and flame-flushed
to these unhingements
these entramplements of gates
Adámic and Eveéic ascendations

Flames be what waters are to me
Soonest incur the fleetest swiftnesses of fire
than cringe to long endurements
far harrowings of waves

And an upswooped evasion-up from hell
remedial to scorn

Risen who water-drenched
by not wild river's soars
Risen who only fired-heart
rumbles and who flames

IV

Had been dry gully that besieged
Had been torrential spawning of my will

to a niágaral bursting-forth as He
And risen know mortality   Know it

by all vein-beatings by pulsings of the heart
by heavings of the knees by bucklings of the eyes

by all out-spoutments of the blood
And open-mouthed expansive to gulárities

of body and of flood
find past all passings

past fallen tower and the broken
past bell-tower clangor and alarm

past bondage past the silence
that lefting path's extolled-emblazonries

and riancies of home
incised incestuous to rock

V

Wherefore ensconcement of this more-than-garden-home
except a paradísian concealment from corsaíring seas

except imperious enshrinement for exilic sons
Gardened enchapeled and enhomed

stand to the cypresses grown greater than cathedrals
stand to the darkest blessings of these trees

that child-hands of my father dug before
ascendant thoughts of leaving or beloving

Stand now to sighing of these trees
and to outswoopments-out to yesterdays

and to enyoked dominions of tomorrows
as if God's breath bequeathed

Yióka moú! Yié moú!
Your seeds are scattered over earth

Oí! How to live
Oimé! And how to be remembered

Spartáric

Thíra

Naked I gleaming came
Oil laved to god
Bold boundless danced all proud

Leaped pure rich bodied
To piercing glory his
Then plied and plunder forced then

Forked by pounding glory theirs
Mind spun stunned body bled
Tongued lipped all mouthed

Till breathing deep deep tasted
Thick odor spilled aboral
Deep spored torrential hot

While from far depths
Upwelled to cratered mouth
Gorge that not long endured

Fire no nor odor taste but scourged
Scarped crag till red roofed
Issue uncontaining cast

And tremble screamed
And paean hurtled
O

O all my
Blood laved body
To Apollo

II

Vineyards

Dancer defiled to him
Longer not basely pierced
Soul spill to Lord

I Michael wings unfold
Stephánic kneel to stones
White naved guard

Carnal terrace that consumed
Lay not this unto them
Unto myself assume

Purge panting dance devotions
Oiled gleamings poundings prayers
And high crag graved

Sight pits light welled
Stigmatic soil's air stones
Mine mine the world's

Pounce dizzy to parched rings
Thick wound coronas
Crouch sprawled below

And bellow spill weep tears
Sweep drench suck hold
Couch dry depressions

As held thorned crown
These vineyards
Throning earth

III

Phíra

Cragsman I fly swift down
Touch vines man wreathed
Man twisted twirled to crowns

Low grown to white air earth
Fox buffeted by winds
Uniquest pillage of wind force

That blunder breaks the grapes
Permits yet inner jewels corolla hang
And golden flourish full

Black twiner of the vines
I stomp stomp grapes
Pour blood to roots to root

The ever coming of the wine
Winds come night come to throe
By Him cause thrown to me

Wires twang to overwhelm
Winds whine man hollowed heart
Aged beginnings of the new begun

Mix mixed with them
I fly on rending wings of wind
And gather gulp gulp wind

That nostrils fill and spill
Inheritance in me my leaping
O my tabernacled heart

IV

Sea

Lone stand to wind
Large loom
Larger than largest life

And blown in me and shown
Tomorrow's seas volcanoes
Largess is mine

To know mine infinite
Minuteness
Mutations I endure

Waves flame low low below
As from vast crater lava flow
To panhagíac bless to baptize me

Then then to go down to sea
Blue black to sink
Where not light shines

To wait yet greater rumblings
That dwellings tore
Man lacerated rived

Layers lay veined pressed He
Rising islandic worlds
That sank

As sink I into sea
As sank hoar stones
Sea chanting primal thrones

V

Kaeménes

Sink sink unfathomed
Slink deep to soundless sea
Light starred plunge deep

As in the howling of the wind
The hollowing of waves
This hallowing of sea

And holy rise hold see
Burned islands lordly round
Surrounded by their host

Steeper or seeming awesomer than they
Black islands that from wind stance
Too reached too poured

Wind lava waves to me
See error of the from the far perceived
That circle joined conjoined your

Weddedness to crumbling of the
Wedding loaves the pulverized of Crete
Black barren glowing only here

Lone walking cratered rimmed
Stricken by sun sun struck
Sight my man shadow

Theótic cope pull I far slung
Sprawl stretch long stemmed contort
Scream to plunge back dominion O in me

VI

Mountain

Then then to sound stone
Dance into sulphur heat
Lave burn before steam fissures

O body fanged entire
By not wind burn sea slash
By not man sweep

But sudden stricken all
Flee flee to crush or larger stand
Be powder pounded into stone

Man crater crushed man burned
Wind called sea laved or thorned
Or lava crowned

Stand coupling
Wait emergence of the stone
That in dark day bright night

All sacred come
Leap plunge to Him
Couplings be man's

While great eruptions God's
Crest crater hurled man hacked
I have been slain to gods

Ah but spartáric rise
Large loom loom earth as looms all earth
Majestic mountain of this O my heart

Kraugé

To thirst then after all to quick and quickest quaking of all
altared flesh . . .

    Alter alert the heart and give not body heed to that
    it heaves

    Soul faulter not nor flush nor falter longer not
    nor fall

    But gush to proclamation of all altaring and
    all unebbable

    O all onrushable revulsions ah
    and anoint

    And soul accompanied by dark rebelliousness of nature
    sequester hold

    Revolt to heart that squadroned quashes that repulses
    hearts

Or agonies be agonies of waves that lashing break
are lost

In sea salvations sundered in thunderous columned kisses or in
single swell

My retrograde my rushing my unquellable kraugé
Heave to

Then mind and body soul heave to and be that silent
sea spume

Splashing love to eyes to lashes lips deep slashing deeps of
deepest heart

Spouting to frenzy squalled to quarry swashed fragility of all
necrótic flesh

Yet O and all and still sate seize and quarter give and fiercely
fiercely live . . .

Agáthic

Adumbral yesterday to earth
Not shot-star up   steep-reared from depths
But aired now   born agáthic
Up now   far now
Far-roared and upstart-high
Marauding sun maraud

Dumbed yesternoon to thirst
Lapped uproar-sating was inundation of
Silver water serve-shared to-with black goat
One tree was shade to us
One home one chapel hailed
One sea one sand one stone

Loined yesternight to sleep
Rat orts snake dung shook-swept to moon
Self   wife   sons
Mitigated mould-corrupted room
Sheet-tossed and blanket-wrapped
Sleep-sprawled to sleep

And thunderous keraunoídial recallings

Goat
Sea-fearing that green droppings dropped when boarding
    boat
Goat's
Drachma-bearing 'not enough for slaughter'
White milk outpoured white milk for milk for cheese

Green sun
That shimmer-shone in stagnant water footed to the cliff
Green sun's
Corrosion into green coined in child's hand
Coined-leaving of progenitors or of lost barbarous ma-
    rauders

Abóma
Sightless-faring slither-poised and bound between smooth
    boulders
Abóma's
Graven culmination in three in thirty days to
    resurrection
Blank eyes to wait to want to crave to see to crave
    to catch the sun

Red moon
That tremble-shone in startled air breasted to the sky
Red moon's
Ascension into red poured in man's hand
Poured-blundering of percursors or of lost undulant
    invaders

72

Trágos
Hair-horning   milkless   male-reeking   purposing
   to plunder
Trágos'
Diminuation of the self to orts   orts of the rat-goat-
   snake
Green coined and splendid-sprawled abominations of
   the fathers

And thunderous keraunoídial returnings

III

Abómal plunge to dawn
Not longer night-assailed
But bright now   dayed now   self-assailed
Sunder thanótic smile that splayed
To arrogance of agonized limbed sprawling
Devouring sun devour

Saffroned effulgent sun
Eclipse ancestral room in this death's sweep
Beast that slew love abjure
And drink not wine of Pramnos only
But coruscations of all light
And suns on suns appearing

Coruscal sun be clamor-clangor of their hearts
Stay them in dark in day
Cascading sun thorn-crown afflatus in the sons
And sons now   shorne of father   only selves
Agáthic   propheted   deep-thorned   pervade
The sun   The sun   The sun

Apherétic

Was it the green of leaf
or whitest water-grief on green
that rattled silver in these hands
as I gave sons to drink

Who was it Lord I kissed
as I touched lips to son
What was it Lord I saw
that made me tremble spill

Whose joy whose innocence was this
that sundered from the plant
was cast upon my bed
a basil-scent a dew

What was the ark I knew
careened from shuttered dark
a blossoming of cactus
a blundering of cross

What was that lanky hell
that swooped to overwhelm
that clawed these man-teats
clawed these lips

What was that scarped desire
that burrowed in this heart
what the blue bead
that mutilated chest

What was the hell I knew
that surged to scar these lips
to gouge these man-teats
suck this blood

Whose joy whose agony was this
that raled from the heart
was cast upon my bed
a rattling a death

Who was it Lord I kissed
as I ark-ached to her
What was it Lord I saw
that made me mausoleumed live

Was it anemone of eyes
or witness of her hands
that rocked to lipping wisdom
announced a covenant in me

With Open Love

There was great purpose in our going down.
Harp, sackbut hardened
Shadrach, Meshach and Abednego
To sweep the salamander stream.
My Shadrach's eyes, bigger and darker, swifter,
Lit on the flitting beast that
Called, commanded us to come.
>Given the time on earth,
>He too would learn to walk.

Sounds of the cornet and the flute
Cracked from their salamander throats.
Cries of the psaltery water
Splashed to our crashing feet.
My Shadrach's hands and Meshach's,
Stretched to the twisting beast
That culled, arrested us in flight.
>Given the time in water,
>He too would learn to swim.

There was great purpose in our going down.
Harp, sackbut softened
Shadrach, Meshach and Abednego
To loose their tightening grip.
My Meshach's voice, higher and stronger, swifter,
Cried for the fleeing beast,
That we not crush its tail.
>Given the time in air,
>He too would learn to breathe.

Barks of the cornets and the flutes
Blasted our eyes, our throats,
Tore at our wavering hands
As salamander slid beneath the mud.
Our blond Abednego, and Shadrach,
Saw that the twisting waters
Swirled, swept to flame.
          Given the time in fire,
          He too would learn to live.

Strung dulcimer, strike the
Gold-image-bearing-king.
Hide, Salamander. Burn deep the
Pristine chambers of the brain. But let our
Shadrach, Meshach and Abednego
Go, go, with open love.
This is no dunghill, but our heart.
          Earth, water, air and fire,
          Be all. Be all as we.

Logos

I know that Pentheus was hacked to pieces by exuberance of his priestess-mother and her tribe, I know that Euripides was torn to pieces by wild dogs, I know that innocent Astyanax was ripped in infant-batterment against the Trojan walls, I know the ripping deaths of bombs and of machines, and so I know a (sundering), a (tearing)—I know a sparagmós, an ancient word which means, in modern Greek, a (wailing). I know like-words like spárgo (swathing), spargáo (swelling to bursting), —and these words, sparagmós, spárgo, spargáo, compelled me use two words in poems, once to a title, "Spartáric", once to a mourning-time, "spartarizmátic".

But when did I first know these words, spartáric, spartarizmátic? Not from some knowledge of Greek culture, not from a thorough knowledge of the classics. It was an oral knowledge first. It was ensightment.

It was hooked fish, that, bleeding from the mouth, fought throbbingly, to die before my eyes. It was a silver-gleaming of its scales that throed spasmodically, spartarizmátically, to die. It was my mother's voice that cried, "Ah! Spartarízi!"

But it was all these words and more, that gave me leave to use spartáric, spartarizmátic. It was spátalos (wasteful), it was sparázo (convulsive stirring), it was sparménos (sown), it was spazmós (spasm), it was spazménos (broken), and it was spárti (a yellow-flaming bush that wildly covers mountainsides of Greece), and it was ríza (root), and it was somewhere, something dimly in my mind, the sound, the meaning even of Sparta and all that city meant. It was return of slaughtered warriors, borne on their shields in glory to the mothers. And it was death of my child-sister. It was her dying in my father's arms. It was my mother's threnody held in his emptied

78

arms. It was our Lord upon the cross. It was His sign. It was the sign of fish. It was His death. And was our own.

So with "Rheátic",—with Rhea, who was (mother of the gods), so with rhea (the ramie-plant), so with another rhea (the English usage of this word as a suffix, my usage of this word as a prefix), so with the Greek rheáki (a running mountain stream), so with the classic and the modern rhéo (flow), so with the Spanish and the English arroyo (small stream, or its dry bed; a deep dry gully), and so with the English words rhetoric, diarrhea.

All is a flooding forth. And calling to the Mother-Goddess, and holding to the noun, rheáki, and following the flow, rhéo,—all adjectivally, adverbially, there is a sound of raining in the word, rheátic; there is a knowledge of a reign.

So with "Sotéric" (Saviour). Sóter was held in my mind's heart from chantings of the church; from midnight vigils for our resurrected Sire; from crossings of myself each night before the icon of our home; from those trinític crossings of my pillow in my childhood nights. And here was love, and here was terror, too.

And so with other titles and with other words. So with agáthic (good, innocent), and so kraugé (a cry), and so with trágos (goat, song, tragedy), so keraunoídial (the lightning-bolt, whose sound rings also kérata, the horns of goat, of song, of tragedy again), so Yéros (the name of a Cretan river, but which is also "old man"), and so gerótic (which by a shifting accent becomes from géros, old,—gerós, or strong), and so parthénic (virginal), and so theótic (god), and so thanótic (death), and so necrótic (dead), so Yióka mou! Yié mou! (My son! My son!), and so those universal cries of anguish, Oí! and Oimé!

79

THE AUTHOR

KONSTANTINOS LARDAS was born in Steubenville, Ohio, on August 3, 1927, of parents who had emigrated to America from the Aegean island of Ikaria. He graduated from the University of Pittsburgh in 1950 and received his M.A. from Columbia University in 1951. He is married and the father of three sons: Nicholas Orestes, George Alexander and Stefaní Jason.

For ten years, he managed a family industrial painting and roofing company in Pittsburgh. He returned to studies in Comparative Literature at the University of Michigan in 1960.

A writer of short stories as well as poetry, Mr. Lardas won a major *Hopwood Award* and an *Atlantic Monthly* "First", in 1961. He received a Fulbright Grant and he and his family spent 1962-1963 in Greece.

He is presently a Predoctoral Instructor with the English Department of the University of Michigan.

THE BOOK

The text of this book was set on linotype in a typeface called PRIMER, a type cut by Rudolph Ruzicka. Ruzicka, a quality wood-engraver and book-designer, cut the type in 1947 at the request of *Linotype*. The attempt to produce a truly-up-to-date legibility face for a variety of needs resulted in the first size in metal, 12 pt., in 1949.

The book was composed and printed by THE ANN ARBOR PRESS, INC., Ann Arbor, Michigan; bound by THE DECKER BOOK BINDERY, Grand Rapids, Michigan. Typography by George A. White; slipcover drawing by Michael Wentworth.

Slipcover photograph by Stuart Wiitala.